Copyright © 2024 Peter Forte

All rights reserved, including the right of reproduction in whole or in part in any form
Illustrator extraordinaire, Ben Silverstein
Created in Canada
ISBN 978-1-7774091-2-8

for grandma,
from grandma

There is this thing called time that's attached to all the moments we share

Moments that were, moments that are, moments that are yet to be there

What I have learned is that time itself is both precious and fleeting

We sometimes say goodbye when it feels like we are only just meeting

I also learned we all have power
to make our sour moments feel sweet

For even on the darkest days,
you made me feel complete

Our time together was such a gift,
even with so much left to pursue

As there were so many things I wanted
to do, that I wanted to do with you

I wanted to play hide and seek,
read books and sing songs

I wanted to teach you life's lessons,
like what's right and what's wrong

I wanted to hear about your dreams,
go skipping hand-in-hand

We were set to be the best of friends,
but time had other plans

I'm sorry I had to go,
but know I'm always here

It may feel like I'm far away,
but you'll learn I'm always near

It really can be hard to grasp,
but sit back and let me try

As I'm no longer a single thing,
but all from root to sky

I'm that fresh cookie scent,
that scrape on your knee

That big belly laugh,
that breeze through the trees

That lick from a dog,
that makes you say yuck

I'm that cute little chicken,
cluckidy-cluck

I'm that moment of sadness,
with no words to say

That moment of joy,
hip-hip-hooray

That line from a book,
that sticks with you forever

I'm that voice in your head,
saying never say never

I'm that flutter in your stomach,
when nerves run high

That feeling of freedom,
that tear in your eye

That mist in the air,
as you stand by the ocean

I'm that time or that place,
that fills you with emotion

This all sounds crazy,
but trust me it's true

As the spirit of me lives
around and in you

I have more examples
to make it all clear

So quiet down please
and listen closely, my dear

Instead of beside,
I'm above and around

Instead of hugs goodbye,
my hugs know no bounds

Instead of my voice,
I speak other ways

Like chirping of birds,
and crashing of waves

Instead of the gardener,
I'm the flowers that bloom

Instead of the chef,
I'm the whole dining room

Instead of the teacher,
I'm the lesson itself

I'm the changing of seasons,
when snow starts to melt

Instead of my humming,
I'm the wind through the chimes

Instead of my words,
I live between the lines

Instead of at bedtime,
I'll see you in dreams

I'll leave you silly messages,
and you'll wonder what they mean

Like dogs that meow, cats that bark,
and fish that say hello

Moo-ing sheep, bah-ing cows,
and mice that fly and glow

They'll make you think,
they'll make you laugh,
they'll make you wonder why

But I hope they'll make you feel safe
and loved when you look up into the sky

A big thing I've learned in life
is that we'll never learn it all

And the best way to live this life
is to keep rising when you fall

Despite all the unknown,
it is important you understand

That I'll always be your rock regardless
of what life has planned

So for all those times that don't make sense, both happy and tragic

For all of life's ups and downs, major moments, and magic

For all the time you wish we had because I left too soon

I'm here,

I'm there,

I'm everywhere,

and forever I'll love you.

Manufactured by Amazon.ca
Bolton, ON